THE PEOPLE WHO LIVED IN BILSTON,

Extracts from the Post Office Directory of Staffordshire, 1864

Edited by Geoffrey Hugh Lindop

Nancy Lindop's The People Who Lived in Staffordshire part 3

First published 2007
Reprinted 2016

Originally published as part of The Post Office Directory of Staffordshire,

Published by:

Mercianotes

Wigton

CA7 5AQ

United Kingdom

© 2016 Mercianotes

ISBN: 978-1530959105

Contents

Signpost-1

Mileage of various towns from Bilston

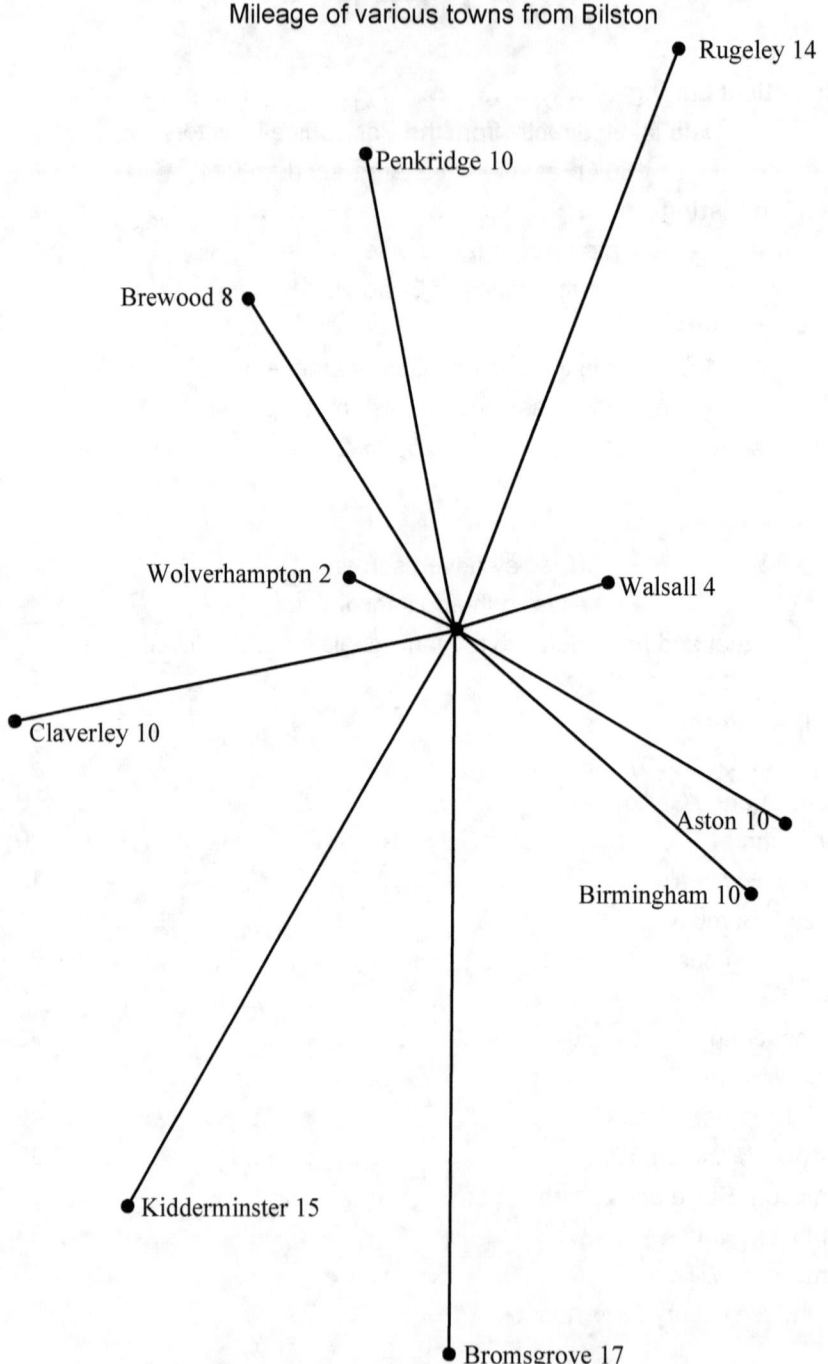

Rugeley 14

Penkridge 10

Brewood 8

Wolverhampton 2

Walsall 4

Claverley 10

Aston 10

Birmingham 10

Kidderminster 15

Bromsgrove 17

Part 1
Alphabetical Listing

Argue Rev. James, Wood Street.

Abbott James, millwright, Ettingshall

Abbott Richard, *Bridge Inn*, & millwright, Coseley Street

Adamson John, hairdresser, 133 Wolverhampton Street

Addison Thomas, butcher, High Street

Adie Francis, grocer & cheese factor, 19 & 21 High Street

Allcorn A. supervisor of the excise, Dudley Street

Anderson George, basket maker, Church Street

Angell Charles, *White Lion*, 38 Temple Street

Ashley Thomas, shopkeeper, Lester Street

Aston James, cooper, Lichfield Street

Aston John, boot & shoe maker, Oxford Street.

Aston William, baker, Crown Street

Attwood Benjamin, milliner, Church Street

Ault Rev. Thomas, Parsonage

Bache David Jones, wine & spirit vaults, High Street

Bacon Charles, tinplate worker, 31 Oxford Street

Bagley Thomas, chemist, High Street .

Bagnall John & Sons, coal & iron masters, Capponfield Iron Works & Colliery

Bailey David, academy, Broad Street

Baker Benjamin Homer, *Union Mill*, Ettingshall

Baker James & William, tinplate workers, Hartshorn Street

Baker John Tomkys, plumber, 147 Oxford Street

Baker John, air tube maker, Thompson Street

Baker John, boot & shoe maker, John Street, New Village

Baker John, *Bell Inn*, 83 Wolverhampton Street

Baker Joseph, *Cricketers Arms*, Church Street

Baker Noah, cabinet maker, Church Street

Baker Samuel, auctioneer, appraiser & building surveyor, High Street

Baker Thomas, grocer & shoemaker, High Street

Baldwin William & Co. ironfounders, engineers & iron masters, Bovereux ironworks

Ball James, *Lamb & Flag*, Salop Row

Banks Joseph, beer retailer, Oxford Street

Barber Frederick, grocer, High Street

Barbors Field Co. coal and iron masters; furnaces & collieries, Highfields & Leasow collieries

Barker Martha (Miss), milliner & dressmaker, Dudley Street

Barley William, dining rooms, Church Street

Barlow Mr. John Chamberlain, Ettingshall

Barlow - see Edge & Barlow

Barnett William, butcher, Oxford Street

Bate John, coal master, Holyhead Colliery

Bates Edwin Joseph, grocer, 127 Wolverhampton Street

Bates Mrs. King Street, Hallfields

Bayliss Moses, blacksmith, Willenhall Road

Bayliss William, beer retailer, Millfields

Baynton Thomas, shoemaker, High Street

Beard Ambrose & Sons, manufacturers of sheet iron, Regent Iron Works

Beard George, iron master, Wellington Street

Beard Mr. Ambrose, Bilston Street, Hallfields

Beard Mr. George, Wellington Street

Beard Mr. John, Hall Street, Hallfields

Beckett Sarah (Mrs.), beer retailer, Temple Street

Beebee Benjamin, plumber, High Street

Beebee Mary (Miss), milliner, Dudley Street

Bennett Joseph, butcher, High Street

Bennett Thomas, wheelwright, Hallfields

Bennett William, butcher, High Street

Best Henry Dewes, surgeon, Lichfield Street

Best Henry Dewes, esq. Wellington Street

Best Herbert, esq. Wellington Street

Best Mrs. Wellington Street

Bew & Kearne, pharmaceutical chemists, Church Street

Billingsley Ann (Mrs.), milliner & dressmaker, Dudley Street

Billingsley William, greengrocer, High Street

Bilston Iron Company, manufacturers of charcoal sheet iron, Factory works

Bilston Old Bank - see William Jones & Sons

Bishop John, linendraper, High Street .

Bishop William, grocer, High Street

Blew John Cardall, solicitor, Church Street

Blocksidge Thomas Benjamin, tobacconist, 18 Oxford Street

Boucher Frederick William, tobacconist, Church Street

Bowen John, clerk to the magistrates, Mount Pleasant.

Bowen Jonathan, grocer, Dudley Street

Bowen Miss, Wellington Street

Bowen Thomas, pawnbroker, Market Street

Bowen William, solicitor, Mount Pleasant

Bowen William, esq. Wellington Street

Bowers William, furniture dealer, Hall Street

Boylin Henry, painter, 14 Dudley Street

Bradbury Ann (Mrs.), provision dealer, Church Street

Bradbury W.J. - see Literary Scientific Institution

Bradley John, wheelwright, Hall Street, Hallfields

Bradshaw George, clog maker, 38 Oxford Street

Breeze Thomas, boot & shoe maker, 17 Wolverhampton Street

Briggs Thomas, cabinet maker, 14 Stafford Street

Brindley John, pipe maker, Bridge Street

Brittain John, iron bucket maker, 22 Chapel Street

Brookes Joseph, leatherseller, Oxford Street

Broughton Robert, beer retailer, Church Street

Brown Charles Gallimore, registrar Oxford Street

Brown Charles G. Esq. Oxford Street

Charles Gallimore Brown

Registrar to the county court at Wolverhampton, solicitor to the Biltong commissioners & local board of health, solicitor to the Bilston gas company, commissioner for taking affidavits in all the courts.

Oxford Street

Brueton Mrs. Mount Pleasant

Bryan William, grocer, 40 Salop Street

Brywood Joseph, beer retailer, Hall Street

Bucknell Robert, excise officer, Dudley. Street

Bullock Charles & Phineas, pawnbrokers High Street

Bullock John, butcher, 52 & 53 Oxford Street

Butler Isaac, grocer & miller, Ettingshall Bridge

Butler John, grocer, High Street

Butler Samuel, *White Horse*, High Street

Butler William, ale & porter brewer & maltster, New Village Brewery

Butler William, grocer, 78 John Street, New Village

Butler William, *King's Head*, Broad Street

Caddick David, butcher, High Street .

Caddick James, brassfounder, Cambridge Street

Caddick Joseph, butcher, Church Street

Caddick Joseph, tinplate worker, 40 Broad Street

Caddick Mary (Mrs.), butcher, Bilston Street, Hallfields

Caddick Silas, butcher, Green Croft

Cadman James, timber merchant, Bilston Road

Cadman James, *Bird in Hand*, High Street

Cadman William, mine agent, Wellington Street

Carter Mr. William, Temple Street

Cave - see Tyler, Cave & Co.

Chambers Hannah (Miss), grocer, Dudley Street

Chambers Thomas, grocer, Temple Street

Chambers Thomas, *Hop Pole*, Dudley Street,

Chaplin Frederick, baker, 25 High Street

Chaplin Walter, baker, Oxford Street

Chappell Edward, clog maker, Oxford Street

Checketts Samuel, ironmonger, Church Street

Chillington Co. (John Turley, manager), Capponfields Iron Works

Choules Woolliscroft, furniture dealers, Oxford Street

Churm Richard, *Golden Cup*, High Street

Claridge Mr. George, Wolverhampton Street

Claridge Mr. Thomas, Mount Pleasant

Claridge North & Co. iron & brass. Founders, Phoenix Foundry

Clark Benjamin, hosier, Church Street

Clarke Edward, *Noah's Ark*, Wolverhampton Street

Clarke Rev. John [Catholic], Oxford Street

Clay John, blacksmith, Catchems Corner

Clossey John, hosier, 19 Oxford Street

Cole George, blacksmith, 50 Hall Street, Hallfields

Cole Isaac, builder Oxford Street

Cole Stephen, mine agent, Wolverhampton Road

Colley James, greengrocer, Mount Pleasant

Collins Mary Ann (Miss), grocer, 32 Hall Street

Compson Thomas, butcher, 42 Hall Street

Coney Thomas, hay & straw dealer, High Street

Conner John, beer retailer, High Street

Cook James, *Plough*, High Street

Cook William, *New Bull's Head*, Wolverhampton Road

Cooksey Thomas, tailor, Railway Street

Cooper Richard, hay & straw dealer, Market Street

Cooper Samuel, corn factor. Wood Street

Corbett Thomas, tailor, 137 Oxford Street

Coslett Mr. Thomas, Dudley Street

Cotrell Alfred, tinplate worker. High Street.

Cottam Thomas, tobacconist, Church. Street

Cox William, grocer, Oxford Street

Cremonini James, upholsterer, Oxford Street

Crooke Charles, wine & spirit vaults, Church Street

Croskery Robert, esq. surgeon, Oxford Street

Cullwick George, baker, Church Street'

Curnock Rev. George [Wesleyan], Church Street

Cutts John, general dealer, 43 Oxford Street

> **John Dean & Son,**
>
> Japanners & manufacturers of iron & papier mache trays,
>
> **Oxford Street & Temple Street.**

Dabbs Samuel, butcher, High Street

Dale William, fruiterer, Church Street.

Dangerfield Joseph, grocer, Dudley Street •

Darbey Mr. William, Wellington Street

Darrell John, coal master, Stonefield Colliery

Davenall James, beer retailer, 5 Brook Street

Davis George, blacksmith, Union Street

Davis John, beer retailer, Coseley Street

Davis William, china dealer, High Street

Day James, farrier, Walsall Street

Dean James Hill, japanner, Wellington Street

Dean John & Son, japanners & manufacturers, Oxford Street & Temple Street.

Delany Patrick, boot & shoe warehouse, Church Street

Delany Patrick, ironmonger, Church Street

Dickinson Thomas, *Seven Stars*, High Street

Duffield Abraham, beer retailer, Salop Street

Dulson Joseph, pork butcher, Church Street

Duman Samuel grocer, Bilston Street

Edge & Barlow, corn millers, Bilston Flour Mills, Ettingshall

Edridge Richard, grocer, Church Street

Edwards Geo. British & foreign timber merchant, Mount Pleasant

Edwards John, carpenter, Oxford Street

Elkington James, *Angel*, Hall Street

Elliott John, wheelwright, Hartshorn Street

Ellis Alexander, grocer, High Street

Elwell John Bassett, boiler maker, Priestfield

Evans Daniel, retail brewer, Market Street

Evans Enoch, *Duke of York*, Bilston Road

Evans William, poulterer, High Street

Faraday Richard, news agent & hairdresser, Oxford Street

Farley George, *Old Bush*, Ward Street, New Village

Farmer James Henry, butcher, Church Street

Farmer Thomas, japanner, Oxford Street.

Fellowes Enoch, tinplate worker, 8 Thames Street

Fellows George, stonemason, Salop Street

Fellows John Edmund, solicitor, Mount Pleasant

Fellows John Edmund, esq. Mount Pleasant

Fellows John, registrar of births, deaths & marriages, 34 Dudley Street

Fellows Mrs. Ward Street

Fellows Philip, engineer & machinist, 73 Oxford Street

Fellows William, butcher, High Street

Fellows William, grocer &c. Ward Street

Firm John, beer retailer, 170 Oxford Street

Fisher Mrs. Wellington Street

Foley Samuel & Co. manufacturers of engine boilers, Bradley boiler works

Forshaw John, linendraper, 27 Oxford Street

Foster Edward, *Spotted Leopard*, Church Street

Fowler Ann, *Horse & Jockey*, 70 Church Street

Fowler Mr. Henry, Ettingshall House

Fowler William, butcher, Church Street

Fox James & Charles, curriers, Oxford Street

Frost Matthew, esq. surveyor, mine & land agent Millfield House.

Furnivall & Williams, ironfounders, Mount Pleasant

Getting John, sheet iron manufacturer Temple Street

Gibbons Benjamin, coal & iron master, Millfield Furnaces

Gilbert Edward, surgeon &c. High Street

Gilbert Edward, esq. High Street

Gilbert Samuel Gillett, surgeon, 16 High Street

Gilbert Samuel G. Esq. High Street

Gray Charles, pharmaceutical chemist, Church Street

Greaves John, plumber &c. 43 Chapel Street

> **Benjamin Gibbons**
>
> coal & iron master, & firebrick manufacturer,
>
> **Millfield Furnaces**
>
> & at Athol House, Edgbaston

Green John Banks, leatherseller, 68 Oxford Street

Green Joseph. engineer, Dudley Street

Green Samuel, mine agent, Wellington Street

Green William, hairdresser, 12 Hall Street, Hallfields

Greenway Joseph, file maker, Hall Street, Hallfields

Griffiths Evan, beer retailer, Mount Pleasant

Griffiths Francis John esq. Wellington Street

Griffiths Francis John, surgeon, Wellington Street

Griffiths John, grocer, Temple Street

Griffiths William, *Swan*, Bilston Street, Hallfields

Grimley Thomas, blacksmith, Broad Street

Groucutt Daniel, esq. Old End House

Groucutt David, esq. Holly cottage

Groucutt Elijah, esq. Coseley Hall

Groucutt Samuel & Sons, ironfounders, Bankfield & Bradleyfield Iron Works

Groucutt Samuel, esq. Rose Hill House

Grove Jabez, hosier, Oxford Street

Guest Elizabeth (Miss), dressmaker, Wellington Street

Guest Joseph, *Waterloo Inn*, 36 Oxford Street

H

Hackett William, stationer, 68 Church Street

Haddon George, plasterer, Dudley Street

Halford Noah, *Black Horse*, High Street

Halford William, grocer, Hall Street, Hallfields

Hall John Willim solicitor, & clerk to the magistrates, Lichfield Street

Hall John Willim, esq. Lichfield Street

Hall Thomas, shopkeeper. Oxford Street

Hall William, *Greyhound Inn*, High Street

Hammond Lavinia (Mrs.), dressmaker, Wellington Street

Hammond Thomas, hairdresser, 131 Oxford Street

Hampson John, baker, Temple Street

Hampton Simeon William, grocer, 158 Oxford Street

Hampton & Co. Ironfounders, Britannia Iron Works

Hancox William Mott, surgeon, 113 Oxford Street

Hancox William Mott, esq 113 Oxford Street

Hands Daniel, watchmaker, 83 Oxford Street

Harding Joseph, grocer & provision merchant, High Street

Hardy James, boot & shoe maker, John Street, New Village

Harper Isaac, saddler, 175 Oxford Street

Harper John, esq. Mount Pleasant

Harper William, currier, Hall Street

Harper & Dickinson, coal masters, Kempson colliery

Harris Isaac, butcher, 63 Bilston Street

Harrison (Wm.) & Pittam (Martha), *White Hart*, 78 Salop Street

Harrisson James, boot & shoe maker, Church Street

Hart William, baker, Oxford Street

Hartill John, greengrocer, Market Street

Haseldine Abraham, *Crown*, Bilston Street

Haseldine William, *Mermaid*, 17 Salop Street

Hateley William, butcher, Church Street

Hatton Wm. esq. Bank, Wellington Street

Hatton Wm. jun. Esq. Ettingshall Villa

Hatton see Thompson, Hatton & Co.

Hawkesford Brothers, mineral brokers, Wellington Street

Hawkweed Ellen (Mrs.), beer retailer, Oxford Street

Hawley James, ropemaker, Oxford Street

Hawley Thomas, ropemaker, Market Street

Hayes John, baker, 119 Oxford Street

Hayward Thomas, shopkeeper, 76 Salop Street

Hayward William, *Navigation Inn*, Salop Street

Heafield Rev. Richard Jewsbury, M.A., [surrogate], Vicarage, Market St.

Henley William, leatherseller, High Street

Hickinbottom Francis, beer retailer, Queen Street

Hickman Edwin, stone & marble mason, Union Street

Hickman Job, grindstone manufacturer & quarry master, Union Street

Hickman John, ironfounder, Wolverhampton Street

Hickman Mrs. Ann, Union Street

Hickman Richard, builder, Market Street

Hilton James Price, butcher, Oxford Street

Hodd Rev. Albert Harry, M.A. Parsonage, Lichfield Street

Holcroft Mr. Francis, Wellington Street

Holcroft Thomas, engineer, Bilston foundry

Holland Joseph, provision dealer, Oxford Street

Holland Thomas, *Swan*, John Street, New Bridge

Hollingsworth Charles, pork butcher, Church Street

Hollingsworth Mary (Mrs.), butcher, Oxford Street

Hollis Charles, tailor, 6 Market Street

Holloway Samuel, timber dealer, Lichfield Street

Holloway Sarah (Mrs.), *Railway Tavern*, Hall Street

Holmes Edmund, beer retailer, Temple Street

Holmes Mary Ann (Miss), day school, Castle Street

Holmes Matthew Matthias, engineer, & manufacturer of screws, Temple St.

Holt Eliza (Miss), shopkeeper, Church Street

Holton Benjamin George, wine & spirit vaults, High Street

Homer William, beer retailer, Wellington Street

Howell Joseph, furniture dealer, Oxford Street

Howell Samuel, plumber & painter, Hall Street

Howell Thomas, boot & shoe maker. 24 Dudley Street

Howes Benjamin, grocer, 78 Church Street

Howes Mary Ann (Mrs.), butcher, Church Street

Howes William, painter & glazier, Stafford Street

Hutchinson Railton, slater, Proudslane cottage

Hyde Ephraim, beer retailer, Spring Vale

Hyde George, wine & spirit vaults, Church Street

Hyde Geo. Spread Eagle & general tinplate worker, Lichfield Street

Hyde Josiah, chemist, 24 Oxford Street

Hyde William, beer retailer, Ward Street

Iddins William, grocer, 13 Wolverhampton Street

Ingram George, grocer, High Street

Isaacs John Lewis tailor & draper, 2 Oxford Street

Ison William, *Red Lion*, George Street

Jackson George, shopkeeper, George Street

Jackson George, hatter, Church Street

Jackson Norfolk Barstow, solicitor, 13 Lichfield Street

Jackson Rev. Wm. [Baptist], Dudley Street

Jackson Thomas, butcher, George Street

James Maria (Miss), dressmaker, George Street

Jevon William, boot & shoe maker, Wood Street

Johnson Joseph, engineer, Wolverhampton Street

Johnson William, beer retailer, Wolverhampton Street

Johnson William, shoe warehouse, 6 Oxford Street

Jones & Bird, japanners, 23 Gozzard Street

Jones & Evans, tailors, Church Street

Jones & Murcott, iron masters, Spring Vale

Jones & Son, bankers, Bilston Old Bank, Lichfield Street

Jones Ann (Mrs.), beer retailer, 86 Oxford Street

Jones Clara (Mrs.), car proprietor, Church Street

Jones David, iron & coal master, Bridge works

Jones Edwin John, *Bull & Mouth*, High Street

Jones Elizabeth (Mrs.), beer retailer Crown Street

Jones Elizabeth (Mrs.), dressmaker, Church Street

Jones Henry, *Vine Inn*, Market place.

Jones John, beer retailer, 76 Oxford Street

Jones John, earthenware dealer, Temple Street

Jones Mary Ann (Miss), hosier, 184 Oxford Street

Jones Samuel, fruiterer, High Street

Jones Samuel, *Roebuck*, Bridge Street

Jones Tabitha (Mrs,), pork butcher, Church Street

Jones Thomas Edmund, grocer, Church Street

Jones Thomas, beer retailer, Thompson Street

Jones Thomas, carter, Church Street

Jones Thomas, japanner, Arthur Street.

Jones William, *Red Lion*, Ettingshall

Kemp John, stationer, Oxford Street

Kempson - see Pratt, Kempson & Simcox

Kendrick David & Son; grocers Oxford Street

Kendrick Sophia (Mrs.), beer retailer, Temple Street

Kent Charles, veterinary surgeon, Union Street

King James, retailer, Oxford Street.

Kirk John, shopkeeper, Pinfold Street

Knight John. beer retailer, 31 Hall Street, Hallfields

Knott James, beer retailer, Lichfield Street

Knowles Thomas James, tinplate worker, Willenhall Road

Lambert George Edwin & Co. chain manufacturers, Priestfield

Lane William, shopkeeper, 8 Brook Street

Langford William, beer retailer, Bridge Street

Langman Alfred, pawnbroker, Church Street

Langston John, grocer, Wolverhampton Street

Lanier John, saddler, Church Street

Larkin Henry William esq., surgeon, 73 Church Street

Larkin John, furniture dealer, High Street

Lathe Whitmer, *Rolling Mill*, Ettingshall

Law Alexander, esq. Wellington Street

Lawley Richard, japanner, Market Street

Leadbetter Charles, printer, Temple Street

Leake Thomas, *Shakspeare Inn*, Market Street

Lee Joseph greengrocer, Oxford Street

Legg George, grindstone mason, Wellington Street

Lester Job Smith, beer retailer, Lester Street

Lester Mary (Mrs.), beer retailer, High Street

Lester Mrs. Lester Street

Lewis Ann (Mrs.), haberdasher Church Street

Lewis Edwin & Frederick, iron merchants, Brook Street

Lewis John Philip, watchmaker, Oxford Street

Lewis John Philip, *Cock Inn,* Willenhall Road

Lewis John, pattern maker, Salop Street

Lewis John, shopkeeper, Ward Street

Lewis William, snuffer tray maker, Mount Pleasant.

Lewis William, *Hand & Keys,* Wolverhampton Street

Lidington George, chemist, High Street

Light James, ironfounder, 164 Oxford Street

Linney Joseph, pork butcher, 162 Oxford Street

Lister Jacob Stanley, timber merchant, Porthouse Bridge

Literary Scientific Institution (W.J Bradbury, hon. Sec.), The Baths, Hall St.

Lloyd Edward, shopkeeper, Wolverhampton Street

Lloyd Jane (Mrs.), *The Swan,* Church Street

Lloyd John Slater, *Castle Inn*, 78 Church Street

Lloyd Richard, *Union Inn*, 44 Coseley Street

Lodge David, chemist, 63 Oxford Street

Lovett Eli, grocer & confectioner, Church Street

Lunn Abraham, beer retailer, Oxford Street

Maddox William, bootmaker, 158 Church Street

Maginity Lawrence, grocer, Oxford Street

Magnus Lewis, marine store dealer, 179 Oxford Street

Mapson Ann, druggist, High Street

Marsh John, corn merchant, 128 Oxford Street

Marston John, japanner, London works, Lester Street.

Mason John, solicitor, 28 High Street

Masters William George, *Lion hotel*, Church Street

Matlow James, blank tray maker, Pipe's Meadow

Mattocks William, confectioner, High Street

Maullin Maria (Mrs.), beer retailer, 174 Oxford Street

Maxfield William, beer retailer, Bradley

Maybury Henry, beer retailer, Wolverhampton Street

Maybury Joseph, beer retailer, Ettingshall Street

Maybury Mary Ann (Mrs.), clothier, High Street

Mayer Henry, grocer, Dudley Street

Mayer Henry, hairdresser, High Street

Merrick James, beer retailer, Broad Street

Merris Richard, bell hanger, Walsall Street

Millar Robert Douglas, linendraper, Church Street

Miller Stephen, milliner, 17 Oxford Street

Millington George, shopkeeper, 17 Queen Street, Hallfields

Millington George, tailor, Church Street

Millington Richard, beer retailer, John Street, New Village

Mills John, mine agent, Dudley Street

Mills Sarah (Miss), grocer, High Street

Millward Abraham, mine agent, Dudley Street

Millward Abraham, jun., mining surveyor, Mount Pleasant

Milward Mr. William, 146 Oxford Street

Moore Robert, grocer, Priestfield

Morewood & Co. iron masters, Ettingshall Iron Works

Morgan George Mortimer, grocer, Oxford Street

Morgan George Mortimer, shoe warehouse, Oxford Street

Morgan Sarah (Mrs.), maltster, Oxford Street

Morrell Maria (Mrs), pawnbroker, Hall Street

Morrell Theophilus, boot & shoe maker, Church Street

Morrell & Griffiths, auctioneers, Church Street

Morris Charles Martin, bootmaker, Temple Street

Morris Rev. Samuel [Primitive Methodist], Dudley Street

Morris William, butcher, High Street

Morris William, galvanized & sheet iron worker 22 Wolverhampton St.

Mudie Mr. John, Wellington Street

Mumford William, Shopkeeper, 7 Salop Street

Nash John, blacksmith, Hartshorn Street

Nash William, wheelwright, Oxford Street

Naylor Samuel, poulterer, Hall Street, Hallfields

Neale Thomas Leaver, hatter & tailor, Church Street

Neast Robert, baker, Chapel Street

Needham George, shopkeeper, John Street, New Village

Newbolt Rev. Hy. Fres. M.A. Vicarage, Bilson

Newell George, butcher, Church Street

Newnes Thomas, boot & shoe maker, Swan bank

Newton John, gunlock smith, Ettingshall

Nicklin & Baker, furnace builders, Wellington Street

Nightingale James, shoemaker, High Street

Nixon Peter, beer retailer, Bridge Street

Nokes Francis, jun. printer & stationer, Church Street

Nokes Francis, sen. printer Lichfield Street

North Mary (Mrs.), grocer, Stafford Street

North William, cabinet maker, Stafford Street

North, John & Son plumbers & painters, Temple Street

Nowland John, general dealer, 17 Oxford Street

Owen Ann Fellows (Mrs.), beer retailer, Ettingshall Bridge

Page Mr. John, Dudley Street

Page William, coal agent, Wellington Street

Palser Ann (Miss), ladies' school, Broad Street

Pardon Joseph, shopkeeper, Bristol Street

Parker Mary (Mrs.), pawnbroker, Dudley Street

Parker William, beer retailer. Goazard Street

Parker William, *Blank Makers Arms* 55 Greencroft

Parkes Edward, pawnbroker, 35 Oxford Street

Parton William, mine agent, George Street

Pea Elizabeth (Mrs.), *Royal Oak,* 83 Salop Street

Pearce James, linendraper, High Street

Pearson Mr. Richard, Mount Pleasant

Pearson Peter, shopkeeper, 32 Queen Street

Pearson Richard, butcher, 152 Oxford Street

Peck William, wine & spirit merchant, Oxford Street

Perkins Thomas, retail brewer, 176 Oxford Street

Perren Ann (Mrs.), confectioner, Church Street

Perry Henry, *Anchor*, Queen Street

Perry Samuel, *Himley Arms*, Dudley Street

Perry Thomas & Son, ironfounders, Highfield works

Pilsbury William, boot & shoe maker, Ward Street. New Village

Pinfield Richard, *White Lion*, Millfields

Pitman - see Harrison (Wm.) & Pittam (Martha)

Pittam Charles, grocer, 10 Brook Street

Plant Henry, wine & spirit vaults, Oxford Street

Plant Walter & Co. wine & spirit vaults, Church Street

Poole Thomas, shopkeeper, 48 Bilston Street

Pope Frederick Alexander, grocer, Hall Street, Hallfields

Pratt William, grocer, High Street

Pratt, Kempson & Simcox, grocers, Church Street

Preston Mr. Frederick W. Oxford Street.

Price Elijah, *White Rose*, Church Street

Price James, beer retailer, Pinfold Street

Price Thomas, butter dealer, Broad Street

Price Thomas, *Globe*, Mount Pleasant

Procter Thomas, boot & shoe maker, Hall Street

Proud Thomas, *Ship & Rainbow*, Oxford Street

Pugh Edward, esq. Church Street

Pumphrey Samuel, boat builder, Millfields

Purcell Edward, hosier, Church Street

Purslow Henry, hairdresser, 145 Oxford Street

Purslow William, beer retailer, Temple Street

Radford Robert, ale & porter agent, Wolverhampton Street

Ralph James, grocer, Cemetery Road

Ramsay Ann (Mrs.), dining rooms, Church Street

Reade George, *Anchor*, High Street

Richards Ann (Mrs.), beer retailer, St. Luke's Street

Richards David, beer retailer, High Street

Richards Rev. Charles William, M.A., Parsonage, Ettingshall

Richards Thomas, surveyor, Church Street

Riley David, upholsterer, Oxford Street

Riley Isaac, beer retailer, 25 Chapel Street

Riley Thomas, undertaker & beer retailer. Wood Street

Riley Thomas, jun. Carpenter, Temple Street

Riley William, builder, Tame Street.

Riley & Waite, ropemakers, 12 Oxford Street

Robinson Thomas, *Wheatsheaf*, Oxford Street

Rogers John, collector of Queen's taxes, Hall Street

Rogers John, *Great Western Inn*, Hall Street

Rogers William, hairdresser, Church Street

Rollason David & Benjamin, wire manufacturers, Bradley works & Porthouse Bridge

Roper Ambrose, *Dog & Partridge*, 23 Broad Street

Rose James, publisher of the '*Iron Trade Guide*', Batman's Hill works

Rose Thos. iron & coal master, Millfields, & Bradley New ironworks

Rose William, iron master, Batman's Hill Ironworks

Rowbotham Thomas, beer retailer, Mill Lane

Rowland George, chimney sweeper, Market Place

Rowley James, japanner & blank tray manufacturer, Mount Pleasant

Rowley Thomas, tinplate worker, Church Street

Rowley Thomas, *Saddle & Stirrup*, 56 Oxford Street

Sale Richard, *Balloon*, High Street

Samuel Philip, outfitter Church Street

Sankey Joseph, blank tray manufacturer, Dudley Street

Sankey Mr. Joseph, Dudley Street

Sankey Thomas, shopkeeper, 27 Coseley Street

Sansom Joseph, builder, Broad Street & Oxford Street

Sansom Stephen. Builder, Church Street

Satterthwaite Alfred, greengrocer, High Street

Satterthwaite Henry, shopkeeper, Church Street

Satterthwaite William, butcher & fishmonger, 75 Church Street

Savings Bank Association (Edward S. Shelley, manager), 46 Church St.

Seahury Thomas, tailor, Pipe's Meadow

Sellman Samuel, timber merchant, Millfields & Penn.

Shakspeare Paron, sheet iron worker, 7 Broad Street

Shale Joseph, beer retailer, Temple Street

Shale Thomas, *Three Tuns*, Bridge Street

Shelley Edward & John, chemists, Church Street

Shelley, Edward - see Savings Bank Association

Shepherd Isaac, grocer, Bristol Street

Sherry Jane (Mrs.), *Old Bush*, 101 Wolverhampton Street

Shipman Richard solicitor, Lichfield Street

Shipman Richard, 64. Lichfield Street

Simcox - see Pratt, Kempson & Simcox

Skemp Robert, milliner, High Street

Slater David, grocer, 26 Oxford Street

Slater Samuel, bootmaker, Temple Street

Smart William, greengrocer, High Street

Smith Edward, grocer, 100 Wolverhampton Street

Smith George & Co. Japanners, Pipe's Meadow works

Smith Isaac & Co. Japanners, Oxford Street

Smith John, beer retailer, Brook Street

Smith John, general dealer, Wolverhampton Street

Smith John, *Royal Exchange*, Salop Street

Smith Joseph, grocer, 82 Oxford Street

Snape Joseph, linendraper, Church Street

Southall John, grocer, 34 Hall Street

Southall Josiah, blacksmith, Temple Street

Sower Edward, shopkeeper, John Street, New Village

Sower Mary Ann (Mrs.), beer retailer, Ward Street

Sparrow, William & J. S. & Co. Ironmasters, Bilston Ironworks

Spence John, linendraper, High Street

Spittal James, shopkeeper, Temple Street

Stahl Juliaus, painter & glazier, 7 Market Street

Stanley George, watchmaker, Church Street

Stephens Edmund, chemist, 18 Hall Street, Hallfields

Stevens Henry, *Talbot Inn*, Oxford Street

Stock Abraham, academy, Mount Pleasant

Stock Caroline (Miss), ladies' school, Mount Pleasant

Stringer Frederick, pianoforte dealer, Church Street

Sykes Joseph, tailor, 21 Stafford Street

T

agg Edwin, baker, Oxford Street

Tate John, beer retailer Ward Street

Tate Joseph, grocer, 28 Queen Street, Hallfields

Taylor Elizabeth (Mrs.), wine & spirit merchant, Church Street

Taylor Joseph, beer retailer, Ettingshall

Taylor William Riley, civil engineer, Lichfield Street

Taylor William, bootmaker, Church Street

Terry Rev. James [Catholic], Oxford Street

Thomas Mr. James, Wellington Street

Thompson David & Josiah, ironfounders, 6 & 8 Temple Street

Thompson David, *Brown Jug*, Temple Street

Thompson Elizabeth (Mrs.), china & glass warehouse, Church Street

Thompson Harriett (Mrs.), dressmaker, Oxford Street

Thompson James, grocer, 83 Church Street

Thompson James, hairdresser, Church Street

Thompson John Henry, painter, Oxford Street

Thompson Maria (Mrs.) stamp office, Wellington Street

Thompson Mrs. Wellenhall Road

Thompson Mr. Richard, Lichfield Street

Thompson Richard, butcher, High Street

Thompson Richard, ironfounder, Pothouse Bridge

Thompson, Hatton & Co. manufacturers of charcoal tinplates, Highflelds

Thorneycroft George B. & Co. coal & iron masters, Bradley Colliery

Thorne, & Thompson, manufacturers of telegraph wire, Bradley ironworks

Tipper Joseph, *Bull's Head Inn*, Church Street

Tippetts Spencer Cooke, collector of town rates, Wellington Street

Tizara Charles, *Ball Court*, 1 Stafford Street

Tomkys John Law, chemist, 140 Oxford Street

Tomkys John Law, wine & spirit vaults, Lichfield Street

Tomkys Susannah (Mrs.) Pawnbroker, 10 Oxford Street

Tomkys William Pool, *Waggon & Horses*, Oxford Street

Torley John, clockmaker, Oxford Street.

Townsend George Hill, solicitor, Tame Street

Townsend William, shopkeeper, Wolverhampton Street

Turley, John - see Chillington Co

Twigg Thomas, boot & shoe maker, 84 Church Street

Tyler, Cave & Co. boot & shoe makers, Church Street

Udall Francis, beer retailer, Oxford Street

Unitt John, tobacconist, High Street

Vaughan Mary Elizabeth (Miss), seminary, Wellington Street

Vickers John, beer retailer, Ettingshall Bridge

Waldron Samuel, varnish manufacturer, Cambridge Street

Waite - see Riley & Waite

Walker Edward, saddler, 160 Oxford Street

Walker Edward, *Angel*, Priestfield

Walker Richard, beer retailer, 74 Oxford Street

Wall Ann (Mrs.). *Swan Inn*, Bradley

1864 Viewpoint

The inhabitants, according to the census of 1861 amounted to 24,364 ; the area is 2,580 acres; the annual value o f assessed property was £61,485.

Wall Joseph, grocer, Market Street

Wallet Thomas, greengrocer, Wolverhampton Street

Walters Ambrose, japanner, Temple Street

Walton George, hairdresser, 160 Oxford Street

Walton Thomas, clog maker, 2 Union Street

Ward Edward, *Old Bull's Head*, & inland revenue office, High Street

Ward William & Sons, iron masters, Priestfield

Warren Frederick, butcher, Church Street

Waterhouse Thomas, solicitor, Mount Pleasant

Waterhouse Thos. esq. 25 Mount Pleasant

Watton Richard, corn & flour dealer, Ettingshall

Watts John, grocer, Oxford Street

Weaver Thomas, staymaker, High Street

Webster John, pork butcher, Church Street

Wedge John, provision dealer, High Street

Wellings Benjamin, dining rooms, 32 Oxford Street

Wells Johnson, esq. Wellington Street

Wells Samuel Johnson, ironmaster, Wellington Street

White Henry, plumber & painter, Lichfield Street

White John, carter, Stafford Street

White Thomas, chemist, Church Street

Whitehead Edward, grocer, 50 & 51 Oxford Street

Whitehead John Poolton, blank tray maker, Bow Street

Whitehouse Henry Bickerton, ironmaster, Prior Field Iron Works

Whitehouse John, painter, 68 John Street, New Village

Whittaker Henry Aspland, carpenter, High Street

Whittaker John, clog maker, 157 Oxford Street

Whittle Thomas, saddler, High Street

Wilks George, hairdresser, 40 Salop Street

Willday George, haberdasher, 16 Oxford Street

Willett, Sarah (Mrs.), *Wellington Inn*, Price Street

Williams Frederick Kempster, boarding & day school, Pipe Hall School

Williams Mr. Henry, Wellington Street

Williams William, *Samson & Lion*, Green Croft

Willim John, esq, Lichfield Street

Willim & Hall, solicitors, Lichfield Street

Wilson Benjamin, pawnbroker, 47 & 48 Temple Street

Windsor Giles, grocer & draper, High Street

Winsper Thomas, beer retailer, Green Croft

Wood Littleton, beer retailer, 27 High Street

Wood Thomas, boat builder, Ettingshall Hall

Woolley John, hairdresser, High Street

Wootton George, shoemaker, Church Street

Wormington Benj. collector of poor rates 22 Wellington Street

Wormington Sarah (Mrs.), seminary, 22 Wellington Street

Worrell Thomas, cooper, High Street

Worton Aaron, bootmaker, Dudley Street

Wright Arthur, *Crown & Cushion*, Bilston Street, Hallfields

Wright Charles, *Queen's Arms*, Wellington Street

**ardley John,** butcher, Oxford Street

---

1864 Viewpoint

The church of St. Leonard was rebuilt in 1827, and is situated in Lichfield-street, at the extreme end of the town, nearest Wolverhampton; it is a very neat edifice, in the Grecian style, with low tower, and adorned with modern clock and belfry: the inside is very commodious and tastefully arranged, containing a fine-toned organ, and a splendid altar-piece, 20 feet by 16, in a massive gilt frame, representing our Saviour taking little children in his arms and blessing them. The living is a perpetual curacy, value £635 per annum, with residence, in the gift of the inhabitants; the incumbent is the Rev. Horatio Samuel Fletcher, B.A. ; the Rev. Albert H. Hodd, M.A., is curate in charge. Attached to the church is a small school for six boys, who are educated and clothed by will of the late Humphrey Perry, Esq.; it is named after its patron, but the affairs are now in Chancery. There are also extensive schools (National) connected with this church, with accommodation for nearly 700, recently erected (by voluntary contributions, aided by the Privy Council,) in the most substantial manner, comprising all recent improvements; the old Cholera Schools are now used by a Working Men's Association. The cholera raged here In 1832, and again in 1849.

Signpost-2

Mileage of various towns from Bilston

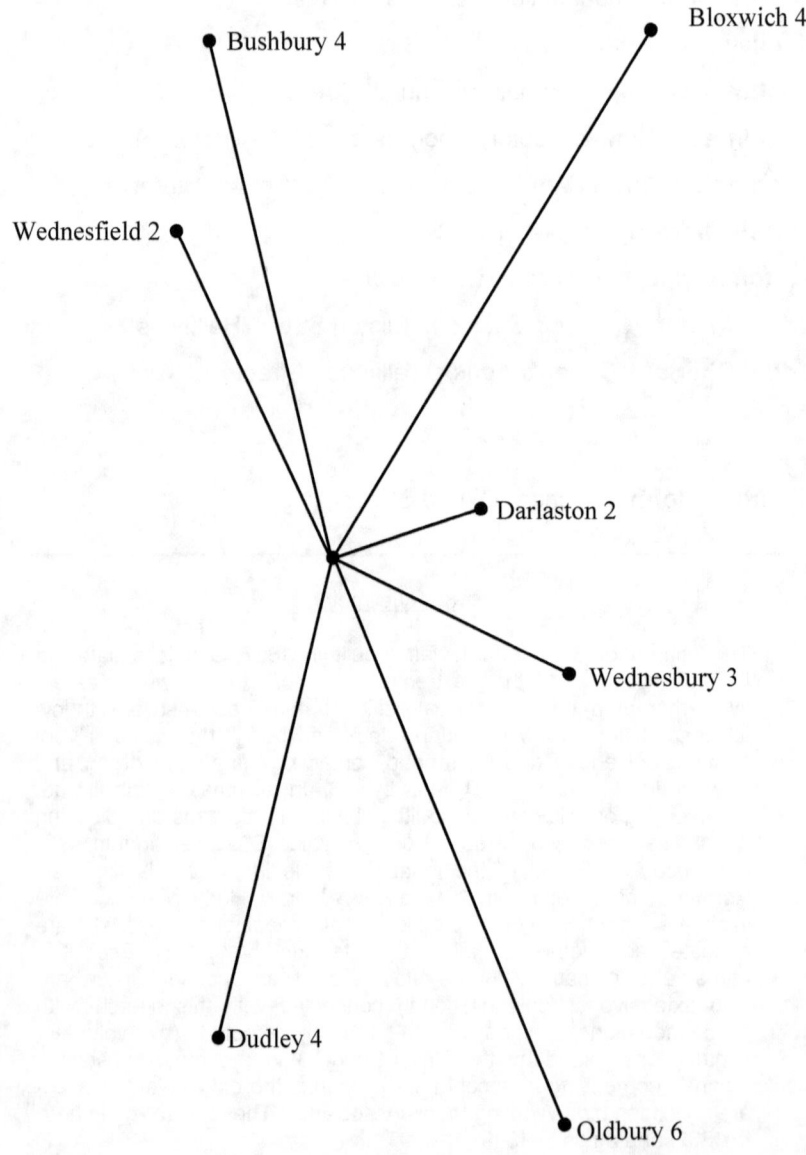

Bushbury 4

Bloxwich 4

Wednesfield 2

Darlaston 2

Wednesbury 3

Dudley 4

Oldbury 6

Part 2
Classified Listing

AIR TUBE MAKERS

Baker John, Thompson Street
Radford Robert, Wolverhampton Street

ALE & PORTER BREWER

Butler William, New Village Brewery

AUCTIONEERS

Baker Samuel, High Street
Morrell & Griffiths, Church Street

BAKERS

Aston William, Crown Street
Chaplin Frederick, 25 High Street
Chaplin Walter, Oxford Street
Cullwick George, Church Street
Hampson John, Temple Street
Hart William, Oxford Street
Hayes John, 119 Oxford Street
Neast Robert, Chapel Street
Tagg Edwin, Oxford Street

BANKERS

Jones & Son, Lichfield Street

BASKET MAKER

Anderson George, Church Street

BEER RETAILERS

Jones Elizabeth (Mrs.), Crown Street
Banks Joseph, Oxford Street
Bayliss William, Millfields
Beckett Sarah (Mrs.), Temple Street
Broughton Robert, Church Street
Brywood Joseph, Hall Street
Conner John, High Street
Davenall James. 5 Brook Street
Davis John, Coseley Street
Duffield Abraham, Salop Street

Beer Retailers - contd.
Firm John, 170 Oxford Street
Griffiths Evan, Mount Pleasant
Hawkweed Ellen (Mrs.), Oxford Street
Hickinbottom Francis, Queen Street
Holmes Edmund, Temple Street
Homer William, Wellington Street
Hyde Ephraim, Spring Vale
Hyde William, Ward Street
Johnson William, Wolverhampton Street
Jones Ann (Mrs.), 86 Oxford Street
Jones John, 76 Oxford Street
Jones Thomas, Thompson Street
Kendrick Sophia (Mrs.), Temple Street

Knight John. 31 Hall Street, Hallfields
Knott James, Lichfield Street
Langford William, Bridge Street
Lester Job Smith, Lester Street
Lester Mary (Mrs.), High Street
Lunn Abraham, Oxford Street
Maullin Maria (Mrs.), 174 Oxford Street
Maxfield William, Bradley
Maybury Henry, Wolverhampton Street
Maybury Joseph, Ettingshall Street
Merrick James, Broad Street
Millington R., John Street, New Village
Nixon Peter, Bridge Street
Owen Ann F. (Mrs.), Ettingshall Bridge
Parker William, Goazard Street
Price James, Pinfold Street
Purslow William, Temple Street
Richards Ann (Mrs.), St. Luke's Street
Richards David, High Street
Riley Isaac, 25 Chapel Street
Riley Thomas, Wood Street
Rowbotham Thomas, Mill Lane
Shale Joseph, Temple Street
Smith John, Brook Street
Sower Mary Ann (Mrs.), Ward Street
Tate John, Ward Street
Taylor Joseph, Ettingshall
Udall Francis, Oxford Street
Vickers John, Ettingshall Bridge
Walker Richard, 74 Oxford Street
Winsper Thomas, Green Croft
Wood Littleton, 27 High Street

BELL HANGER

Merris Richard, Walsall Street

BLACKSMITH

Bayliss Moses, Willenhall Road
Clay John, Catchems Corner
Cole George, 50 Hall Street, Hallfields
Davis George, Union Street
Grimley Thomas, Broad Street
Nash John, Hartshorn Street
Southall Josiah, Temple Street

BLANK TRAY MAKERS

Matlow James, Pipe's Meadow
Rowley James, Mount Pleasant
Sankey Joseph, Dudley Street
Whitehead John Poolton, Bow Street

BOAT BUILDERS

Pumphrey Samuel, Millfields
Wood Thomas, Ettingshall hall

BOILER MAKER

Elwell John Bassett, Priestfield

BOOT & SHOE MAKERS

Ashley Thomas, Lester Street
Aston John, Oxford Street.
Baker John, John Street, New Village
Baker Thomas, High Street
Baynton Thomas, High Street
Breeze T., 17 Wolverhampton Street
Hardy James, John Street, New Village
Harrisson James, Church Street
Howell Thomas, 24 Dudley Street
Jevon William, Wood Street
Maddox William, 158 Church Street
Morrell Theophilus, Church Street
Morris Charles Martin, Temple Street
Newnes Thomas, Swan bank
Nightingale James, High Street
Pilsbury W., Ward Street. New Village
Procter Thomas, Hall Street
Slater Samuel, Temple Street
Taylor William, Church Street
Twigg Thomas, 84 Church Street
Tyler, Cave & Co. Church Street
Wootton George, Church Street
Worton Aaron, Dudley Street

BOOT & SHOE WAREHOUSE

Delany Patrick, Church Street

Thomas Holcroft

Engineer, iron & brass founder & wright, manufacturer of steam engines, chilled & grain rolls & every description of machinery for the manufacture of iron.

Bilston Foundry

BRASSFOUNDER

Caddick James, Cambridge Street

BUILDERS

Cole Isaac, Oxford Street
Hickman Richard, Market Street
Riley William, Tame Street
Sansom J., Broad & Oxford Streets
Sansom Stephen, Church Street

BUTCHERS

Addison Thomas, High Street
Barnett William, Oxford Street
Bennett Joseph, High Street
Bennett William, High Street
Bullock John, 52-3 Oxford Street
Caddick David, High Street
Caddick Joseph, Church Street
Caddick Mary. (Mrs.), Hallfields
Caddick Silas, Green Croft
Compson Thomas, 42 Hall Street
Dabbs Samuel, High Street
Farmer James Henry, Church Street
Fellows William, High Street
Fowler William, Church Street
Harris Isaac, 63 Bilston Street
Hateley William, Church Street
Hilton James Price, Oxford Street
Hollingsworth M. (Mrs.), Oxford Street
Howes Mary Ann (Mrs.), Church Street
Jackson Thomas, George Street
Morris William, High Street
Newell George, Church Street
Pearson Richard, 152 Oxford Street
Satterthwaite W., 75 Church Street
Thompson Richard, High Street
Warren Frederick, Church Street
Yardley John, Oxford Street

BUTTER DEALER

Price Thomas, Broad Street

CABINET MAKERS

Baker Noah, Church Street
Briggs Thomas, 14 Stafford Street
North William, Stafford Street

CAR PROPRIETOR

Jones Clara (Mrs.), Church Street

CARPENTERS

Edwards John, Oxford Street
Riley Thomas, jun., Temple Street
Whittaker Henry Aspland, High Street

CARTERS

Jones Thomas, Church Street
White John, Stafford Street

CHAIN MANUFACTURER

Lambert G. E. & Co. Priestfield

CHEESE FACTOR

Adie Francis, 19 & 21 High Street

CHEMISTS

Shelley Edward & John, Church Street
Bagley Thomas, High Street
Hyde Josiah, 24 Oxford Street
Lidington George, High Street
Lodge David, 63 Oxford Street
Stephens E., 18 Hall Street, Hallfields
Tomkys John Law, 140 Oxford Street
White Thomas, Church Street

CHIMNEY SWEEPER

Rowland George, Market place

CHINA DEALER

Davis William, High Street

CHINA & GLASS WAREHOUSE

Thompson E. (Mrs.), Church Street

CIVIL ENGINEER

Taylor William Riley, Lichfield Street

1864 Viewpoint

The Stour Valley railway passes within 1 mile of the town, and is near the Birmingham and Fazeley canal. The Dudley, Birmingham, and Wolverhampton branch of the Great Western, the station for which is at Pipe's Meadow, and the West Midland railway, pass through the centre of the town, and the Ettingshall station of the London and North Western is near.

CLOCK & WATCHMAKERS

Torley John, Oxford Street
Hands Daniel, 83 Oxford Street
Lewis John Philip, Oxford Street
Stanley George, Church Street

CLOG MAKERS

Bradshaw George, 38 Oxford Street
Chappell Edward, Oxford Street
Walton Thomas, 2 Union Street
Whittaker John, 157 Oxford Street

CLOTHIER

Maybury Mary Ann (Mrs.), High Street

COAL AGENT

Page William, Wellington Street

COAL & IRON MASTERS

Bagnall J. & Sons, Capponfield works
Baldwin W. & Co. Bovereux Ironworks
Barbors Field Co. Highfields Colliery
Bate John, Holyhead Colliery
Beard George, Wellington Street
Darrell John, Stonefield Colliery
Gibbons Benjamin, Millfield Furnaces
Harper & Dickinson, Kempson colliery
Jones David, Bridge works
Jones & Murcott, Spring Vale
Morewood & Co. Ettingshall Iron Works
Wells Samuel J., Wellington Street
Coal & Iron Masters - contd.
Whitehouse H. B., Prior Field Works
Rose Thos. Millfields, New Ironworks
Rose William, Batman's Hill ironworks
Thorneycroft G. B. & Co. Bradley Colliery
Ward William & Sons, Priestfield

CONFECTIONERS

Lovett Eli, Church Street
Mattocks William, High Street
Perren Ann (Mrs.), Church Street

COOPERS

Aston James, Lichfield Street
Worrell Thomas, High Street

CORN DEALERS ETC

Cooper Samuel, Wood Street
Marsh John, 128 Oxford Street
Watton Richard, Ettingshall

CORN MILLERS

Butler Isaac, Ettingshall Bridge
Edge & Barlow, Bilston Flour Mills

CURRIER

Fox James & Charles, Oxford Street
Harper William, Hall Street

DINING ROOMS

Barley William, Church Street
Ramsay Ann (Mrs.), Church Street
Wellings Benjamin, 32 Oxford Street

DRAPERS

Isaacs John Lewis 2 Oxford Street
Windsor Giles, High Street

DRESSMAKER

Barker Martha (Miss), Dudley Street
Billingsley Ann (Mrs.), Dudley Street
Guest Elizabeth, Wellington Street
Hammond Lavinia, Wellington Street
James Maria (Miss), George Street
Jones Elizabeth (Mrs.), Church Street
Thompson Harriett, Oxford Street

DRUGGIST

Mapson Ann, High Street

EARTHENWARE DEALER

Jones John, Temple Street

ENGINEERS

Baldwin W. & Co. Bovereux Ironworks
Fellows Philip, 73 Oxford Street
Green Joseph. Dudley Street
Holcroft Thomas, Bilston foundry
Holmes M. M., Temple Street
Johnson J., Wolverhampton Street

Thompson, Hatton & Co.

Manufacturers of charcoal tinplates,
tin sheets, sheet iron &c. &c.

Bradley Tinplate Works

David Jones

iron & coal master,

Bridge works,

& Herbert's Park works & furnaces, Darlaston

Jones & Son

Bankers
(draw on, Spooner, Attwoods & Co.),
Bilston Old Bank, Lichfield Street

BILSTON IRON COMPANY

Manufacturers of best, best best & charcoal sheet iron & every description of boat & boiler plates, Canada plates, dish plates &c.,

Factory Works

David & Josiah Thompson

Ironfounders, table & chamber snuffer makers & tinmen's furniture manufacturers,

6 & 8 Temple street

William Morris

galvanized & sheet iron worker & manufacturer of all kinds of house shovels,

22 Wolverhampton St.

William Thompson & Son

boiler makers
& iron boat builders
Highfields

William & J. S. Sparrow & Co.

ironmasters,
Bilston Ironworks
& Stow heath, Wolverhampton

EXCISE OFFICER

Bucknell Robert, Dudley. Street

FARRIER

Day James, Walsall Street

FILE MAKER

Greenway J., Hall Street, Hallfields

FISHMONGER

Satterthwaite W., 75 Church Street

FRUITERERS

Dale William, Church Street
Jones Samuel, High Street

FURNACE BUILDER

Nicklin & Baker, Wellington Street

FURNITURE DEALERS

Choules Woolliscroft, Oxford Street
Bowers William, Hall Street
Howell Joseph, Oxford Street
Larkin John, High Street

GENERAL DEALERS

Cutts John, 43 Oxford Street
Nowland John, 117 Oxford Street
Smith John, Wolverhampton Street

GLAZIERS

Howes William, Stafford Street
Stahl Juliaus, 7 Market Street

GREENGROCERS

Billingsley William, High Street
Colley James, Mount Pleasant
Hartill John, Market Street
Lee Joseph Oxford Street
Satterthwaite Alfred, High Street
Smart William, High Street
Wallet Thomas, Wolverhampton Street

GRINDSTONE MASON

Legg George, Wellington Street

GROCERS

Adie Francis, 19 & 21 High Street
Baker Thomas, High Street
Barber Frederick, High Street
Bates E. J., 127 Wolverhampton Street
Bishop William, High Street

Bowen Jonathan, Dudley Street
Bryan William, 40 Salop Street
Butler Isaac, Ettingshall Bridge
Butler John, High Street
Butler W., 78 John Street, New Village
Chambers Hannah, Dudley Street
Chambers Thomas, Temple Street
Collins Mary Ann, 32 Hall Street
Cox William, Oxford Street
Dangerfield Joseph, Dudley Street
Duman Samuel Bilston Street
Edridge Richard, Church Street
Ellis Alexander, High Street
Fellows William, Ward Street
Griffiths John, Temple Street
Halford William, Hall Street, Hallfields
Hampton S. W., 158 Oxford Street
Harding Joseph, High Street
Howes Benjamin, 78 Church Street
Iddins W., 13 Wolverhampton Street
Ingram George, High Street
Jones Thomas E., Church Street
Kendrick David & Son, Oxford Street
Langston John, Wolverhampton Street
Lovett Eli, Church Street
Maginity Lawrence, Oxford Street
Mayer Henry, Dudley Street
Mills Sarah (Miss), High Street
Moore Robert, Priestfield
Morgan George M., Oxford Street.
North Mary (Mrs.), Stafford Street
Pittam Charles, 10 Brook Street
Pope F. A., Hall Street, Hallfields
Pratt William, High Street
Pratt, Kempson & Simcox, Church St.
Ralph James, Cemetery Road
Shepherd Isaac, Bristol Street
Slater David, 26 Oxford Street
Smith Ed., 100 Wolverhampton Street
Smith Joseph, 82 Oxford Street
Southall John, 34 Hall Street
Tate J., 28 Queen Street, Hallfields
Thompson James, 83 Church Street
Wall Joseph, Market Street
Watts John, Oxford Street
Whitehead Ed., 50-51 Oxford Street
Windsor Giles, High Street

Henry Bickerton Whitehouse

ironmaster, ironfounder &
firebrick manufacturer

Prior Field Iron Works

1864 Viewpoint

National schools upon an extensive
scale are open daily, and also for
the Wesleyan Connexion and
Roman Catholics. There are also a
small neat chapel and schools at
Cappon-field, built and entirely
supported by Messrs. John Bagnall
and Sons.

Ambrose Beard & Sons,

manufacturers of all descriptions
of sheet iron,

also paddled steel & iron bars.

Regent Iron Works

GUNLOCK SMITH

Newton John, Ettingshall

HABERDASHERS

Lewis Ann (Mrs.), Church Street
Willday George, 16 Oxford Street

HAIRDRESSERS

Purslow Henry, 145 Oxford Street
Adamson John, 133 Wolverhampton St.
Faraday Richard, Oxford Street
Green William, 12 Hall Street, Hallfields
Hammond Thomas, 131 Oxford Street
Mayer Henry, High Street
Rogers William, Church Street
Thompson James, Church Street
Walton George, 160 Oxford Street
Wilks George, 40 Salop Street
Woolley John, High Street

HATTERS

Jackson George, Church Street
Neale Thomas Leaver, Church Street

HAY & STRAW DEALERS

Coney Thomas, High Street
Cooper Richard, Market Street

HOSIERS

Clark Benjamin, Church Street
Clossey John, 19 Oxford Street
Grove Jabez, Oxford Street
Jones Mary Ann, 184 Oxford Street
Purcell Edward, Church Street

1864 Viewpoint

At Ettingshall, formerly Catchems-corner, stands Trinity church, in Sedgley parish, the greater portion of the inhabitants being, however, in Bilston township. There are extensive schools here connected with the Church for boys, girls and infants. The Rev. C. W. Richards, M.A., of Trinity College, Dublin, is the incumbent. The living is a perpetual curacy, in the gift of the Bishop of Lichfield, annual value, £200. St. Luke's church, in Market street, is a neat stone building in the Early English or First Pointed style, and consists of a nave, 75 feet by 22 feet, north and south aisles, 24 feet by 17feet, a chancel aisle in the north-east and a tower and spire on the south-east of the chancel; there is also a west gallery in the nave for children: the whole church contains 800 sittings, 600 of which are free: it was built at the cost of £4,825, including the vicarage and one school. The living is a vicarage, value £150, in the alternate gift of the Crown and the bishop of the diocese; the Rev. Richard Jewsbury Heafield, M.A., of St. Catherine's College, Cambridge, is the incumbent and surrogate. This district was originally constituted under Sir Robert Peel's Act, and afterwards made a vicarage under the Wolverhampton Deanery Act. There are chapels for Roman Catholics, Baptists, Independents, Wesleyan, Methodist New Connexion, and Primitive Methodists.

IRON BUCKET MAKER

Brittain John, 22 Chapel Street

IRON MERCHANT

Lewis Edwin & Frederick, Brook Street

IRON & BRASS. FOUNDERS

Chillington Co. Capponfields works
Baldwin W. & Co. Bovereux ironworks
Claridge North & Co. Phoenix foundry
Furnivall & Williams, Mount Pleasant
Groucutt S. & Sons, Bankfield Iron Works
Hampton & Co. Britannia Iron Works
Hickman John, Wolverhampton Street
Light James, 164 Oxford Street
Perry Thomas & Son, Highfield works
Sparrow, Wm. & J. S. & Co. Bilston
Thompson David & Josiah, Temple St.
Thompson Richard, Pothouse Bridge

IRONMONGERS

Checketts Samuel, Church Street
Delany Patrick, Church Street

JAPANNERS

Dean James Hill, Wellington Street
Dean J. & Son, Oxford Street
Farmer Thomas, Oxford Street.
Jones Thomas, Arthur Street.
Junes & Bird, 23 Gozzard Street
Lawley Richard, Market Street
Marston John, Lester Street.
Rowley James, Mount Pleasant
Smith G. & Co. Pipe's Meadow Works
Smith Isaac & Co. Oxford Street
Walters Ambrose, Temple Street

LEATHERSELLERS

Brookes Joseph, Oxford Street
Green John Banks, 68 Oxford Street
Henley William, High Street

LINENDRAPERS

Bishop John, High Street
Forshaw John, 27 Oxford Street
Millar Robert Douglas, Church Street
Pearce James, High Street
Snape Joseph, Church Street
Spence John, High Street

MALTSTERS

Butler William, New Village Brewery
Morgan Sarah (Mrs.), Oxford Street

MANUFACTURERS

Beard A. & Sons, Regent Iron Works
Bilston Iron Company, Factory Works
Dean John & Son, Oxford Street.
Foley Sam. & Co. Bradley Boiler Works
Hickman Job, Union Street
Holmes Matthew M., Temple Street
Thompson, Hatton & Co. Highflelds
Thorne, & Thompson, Bradley Ironworks

MARINE STORE DEALER

Magnus Lewis, 179 Oxford Street

MILLINERS

Attwood Benjamin, Church Street
Barker Martha (Miss), Dudley Street
Beebee Mary (Miss), Dudley Street
Billingsley Ann (Mrs.), Dudley Street
Miller Stephen, 17 Oxford Street
Skemp Robert, High Street

MILLWRIGHTS

Abbott James, Ettingshall
Abbott Richard, Coseley Street

MINE AGENTS

Cadman William, Wellington Street
Cole Stephen, Wolverhampton Road
Green Samuel, Wellington Street
Mills John, Dudley Street
Millward Abraham, Dudley Street
Parton William, George Street

MINERAL BROKER

Hawkesford Brothers, Wellington St.

MINING SURVEYOR

Millward Abraham, jun., Mount Pleasant

NEWS AGENT

Faraday Richard, Oxford Street

OUTFITTER

Samuel Philip, Church Street

PAINTERS

Boylin Henry, 14 Dudley Street
Howell Samuel, Hall Street
Howes William, Stafford Street

North, John & Son Temple Street
Stahl Juliaus, 7 Market Street
Thompson John Henry, Oxford Street
White Henry, Lichfield Street
Whitehouse J, John Street, New Village

PATTERN MAKER

Lewis John, Salop Street

PAWNBROKERS

Bullock Charles & Phineas, High St .
Bowen Thomas, Market Street
Langman Alfred, Church Street
Morrell Maria (Mrs), Hall Street
Parker Mary (Mrs.), Dudley Street
Parkes Edward, 35 Oxford Street
Tomkys Susannah, 10 Oxford Street
Wilson Benjamin, 47-48 Temple Street

PHARMACEUTICAL CHEMIST

Bew & Kearne, Church Street
Gray Charles, Church Street

PIANOFORTE DEALER

Stringer Frederick, Church Street

PIPE MAKER

Brindley John, Bridge Street

PLASTERER

Haddon George, Dudley Street

PLUMBERS

Baker John Tomkys, 147 Oxford St.
Beebee Benjamin, High Street
Greaves John, 43 Chapel Street
Howell Samuel, Hall Street
North, John & Son Temple Street
White Henry, Lichfield Street

PORK BUTCHERS

Dulson Joseph, Church Street
Hollingsworth Charles, Church Street
Jones Tabitha (Mrs,), Church Street
Linney Joseph, 162 Oxford Street
Webster John, Church Street

POULTERERS

Evans William, High Street
Naylor Samuel, Hall Street, Hallfields

PRINTERS

Nokes Francis, jun. Church Street
Nokes Francis, sen. Lichfield Street
Leadbetter Charles, Temple Street

PROVISION DEALERS

Bradbury Ann (Mrs.), Church Street
Harding Joseph, High Street
Holland Joseph, Oxford Street
Wedge John, High Street

PUBLIC HOUSES AND INNS

Anchor Perry Henry, Queen Street
Anchor Reade George, High Street
Angel Elkington James, Hall Street
Angel Walker Edward, Priestfield

Ball Court Tizara Charles, 1 Stafford St.
Balloon Sale Richard, High Street
Bell Inn Baker J., 83 Wolverhampton St
Bird in Hand Cadman James, High St.
Black Horse Halford Noah, High Street
Blank Makers Arms Parker W., Greencroft
Bridge Inn Abbott Richard, Coseley St.
Brown Jug Thompson D., Temple St.
Bull's Head Inn Tipper J., Church St.
Bull & Mouth Jones Edwin J., High St.

Castle Inn Lloyd John S., 78 Church St.
Cock Inn Lewis John P., Willenhall Rd.
Cricketers Arms Baker J., Church St.
Crown Haseldine Abraham, Bilston St.
Crown & Cushion Wright A., Bilston St.

Dog & Partridge Roper A., 23 Broad St.
Duke of York Evans Enoch, Bilston Rd.

Globe Price Thomas, Mount Pleasant
Golden Cup Churm Richard, High St.
Great Western Inn Rogers J., Hall St.
Greyhound Inn Hall William, High St.

Hand & Keys Lewis W., Wolverhampton St.
Himley Arms Perry Samuel, Dudley St.
Hop Pole Chambers Thomas, Dudley St.
Horse & Jockey Fowler Ann, Church St.

King's Head Butler William, Broad St.
Lamb & Flag Ball James, Salop Row
Lion hotel Masters W. G., Church St.

Mermaid Haseldine William, 7 Salop St.

Navigation Inn Hayward Wm., Salop St.
New Bull's Head Cook W., Wolverhampton Rd.
Noah' s Ark Clarke E., Wolverhampton St.

Old Bull's Head Ward Edward, High St.
Old Bush Sherry Jane, Wolverhampton St.
Old Bush Farley George, Ward Street,

Plough Cook James, High Street

Queen's Arms Wright C., Wellington St.

Railway tavern Holloway Sarah, Hall St.
Red Lion Ison William, George Street
Red Lion Jones William, Ettingshall
Roebuck Jones Samuel, Bridge Street
Rolling Mill Lathe Whitmer, Ettingshall
Royal Exchange Smith John, Salop St.
Royal Oak Pea Elizabeth, 83 Salop St.

Saddle & Stirrup Rowley T., Oxford St.
Samson & Lion Williams W., Green Croft
Seven Stars Dickinson Thos., High St.
Shakspeare Inn Leake Thos., Market St.
Ship & Rainbow Proud Thos., Oxford St.
Spotted Leopard Foster Ed., Church St.
Swan Griffiths William, Bilston Street
Swan Holland Thomas, John Street
Swan Inn Wall Ann (Mrs.). Bradley

Talbot Inn Stevens Henry, Oxford St.
The Swan Lloyd Jane, Church St.
Three Tuns Shale Thomas, Bridge St.

Union Inn Lloyd Richard, 44 Coseley St.
Union Mill Baker Ben. H., Ettingshall

Vine Inn Jones Henry, Market place

Waggon & Horses Tomkys W. P., Oxford St.
Waterloo Inn Guest Joseph, Oxford St.
Wellington Inn Willett, Sarah, Price St.
Wheatsheaf Robinson Thos., Oxford St.
White Hart Harrison & Pittam, Salop St.
White Horse Butler Samuel, High Street
White Lion Angell C., 38 Temple St.
White Lion Pinfield Richard, Millfields
White Rose Price Elijah, Church Street

QUARRY MASTER

Hickman Job, Union Street

RATE & TAX COLLECTORS

Allcorn A. Dudley Street
Rogers John, Hall Street
Tippetts Spencer Cooke, Wellington St.
Ward Edward, High Street
Wormington Benj. 22 Wellington St

REGISTRARS & CLERKS

Bowen John, Mount Pleasant
Brown Charles Gallimore, Oxford St.
Fellows John, 34 Dudley Street

RETAIL BREWERS

Evans Daniel, Market Street
Perkins Thomas, 176 Oxford Street

ROPEMAKERS

Hawley James, Oxford Street
Hawley Thomas, Market Street
Riley & Waite, 12 Oxford Street

SADDLERS

Harper Isaac, 175 Oxford Street
Lanier John, Church Street
Walker Edward, 160 Oxford Street
Whittle Thomas, High Street

SCHOOLS, ACADEMIES &c.

Bailey David, Broad Street
Holmes Mary Ann , Castle Street
Palser Ann, Broad Street
Stock Abraham, Mount Pleasant
Stock Caroline, Mount Pleasant
Vaughan Mary Elizabeth, Wellington St.
Williams Frederick K., Pipe Hall school
Wormington Sarah, 22 Wellington St.

1864 Viewpoint

A cemetery has been recently opened an easy distance from the town, on the Wolverhampton road, and other improvements are in contemplation. The new baths and washhouses, erected in 1853, front the designs of Messrs. Ashpitel and Whicheord, of London, at an expense, inclusive of the cost of the site, of £2,700, form one of the principal ornaments of the town: the. accommodation • provided is a swimming bath, plunging bath, 23 private baths, and 12 washing stalls ; the building, situated in Hall-street, is the property of a public company, formed for the purpose o! erecting baths and washhouses, town hall. and reading rooms, of which Mr. Charles Griffiths is secretary. There are also News Rooms and a Temperance Hall.

Thomas Perry & Son

Ironfounders, engineers &
manufacturers of brass & iron
bedsteads, fireproof safes, wrought,
iron gates, fencing, hurdles, wire
netting &c.

Highfield works

Also at 21 Coleman Street, London E C

& Renfield Street, Glasgow

John Marston

Japanner, iron & tinplate worker,
Manufacture of papier mache
& iron trays.

London works, Lester street

SHEET IRON MANUFACTURERS & WORKERS

Getting John, Temple Street
Shakspeare Paron, 7 Broad Street

SHOE WAREHOUSE

Johnson William, 6 Oxford Street
Morgan George Mortimer, Oxford St.

SHOPKEEPERS

Hall Thomas, Oxford Street
Hayward Thomas, 76 Salop Street
Holt Eliza, Church Street
Jackson Georgee, George Street
King James, Oxford Street
Kirk John, Pinfold Street
Lane William, 8 Brook Street
Lewis John, Ward Street
Lloyd Edward, Wolverhampton Street
Millington George, 17 Queen Street
Mumford William. 7 Salop Street
Needham George, John Street
Pardon Joseph, Bristol Street
Pearson Peter, 32 Queen Street
Poole Thomas, 48 Bilston Street
Sankey Thomas, 27 Coseley Street
Satterthwaite Henry, Church Street
Sower Edward, John Street
Spittal James, Temple Street
Townsend William, Wolverhampton St.

SLATER

Hutchinson R., Proudslane Cottage

SNUFFER TRAY MAKER

Lewis William, Mount Pleasant

SOLICITORS

Blew John Cardall, Church Street
Bowen William, Mount Pleasant
Fellows John E., Mount Pleasant
Hall John Willim Lichfield Street
Jackson Norfolk Barstow, Lichfield St.
Mason John, 28 High Street
Shipman Richard Lichfield Street
Townsend George Hill, Tame Street
Waterhouse Thomas, Mount Pleasant
Willim & Hall, Lichfield Street

STAMP OFFICE

Thompson Maria (Mrs.) Wellington St.

STATIONERS

Hackett William, 68 Church Street
Kemp John, Oxford Street
Nokes Francis, jun., Church Street

STAYMAKER

Weaver Thomas, High Street

STONEMASONS

Fellows George, Salop Street
Hickman Edwin, Union Street

SURGEONS

Best Henry Dewes, Lichfield Street
Gilbert Edward, High Street
Gilbert Samuel Gillett, 16 High Street
Griffiths Francis John, Wellington St.
Hancox William Mott, 113 Oxford St.
Larkin Henry William, 73 Church St.
Croskerry Robert, Oxford Street

SURVEYORS

Froet Matthew, Millfield House.
Richards Thomas, Church Street

TAILORS

Cooksey Thomas, Railway Street
Corbett Thomas, 137 Oxford Street
Hollis Charles, 6 Market Street
Isaacs John Lewis 2 Oxford Street
Jones & Evans, Church Street
Millington George, Church Street
Neale Thomas Leaver, Church Street
Seahury Thomas, Pipe's Meadow
Sykes Joseph, 21 Stafford Street

TIMBER MERCHANTS

Cadman James, Bilston Road
Edwards Geo. Mount Pleasant

Holloway Samuel, Lichfield Street
Lister Jacob St., Porthouse Bridge
Sellman Samuel, Millfields

TINPLATE WORKERS

Bacon Charles, 31 Oxford Street
Baker James & William, Hartshorn St.
Caddick Joseph, 40 Broad Street
Tinplate Workers - contd.
Cotrell Alfred, High Street
Fellowes Enoch, 8 Thames Street
Hyde Geo. Lichfield Street
Knowles Thomas James, Willenhall Rd.
Rowley Thomas, Church Street

TOBACCONISTS

Blocksidge Thomas B., Oxford St.
Boucher Frederick William, Church St.
Cottam Thomas, Church. Street
Unitt John, High Street

UNDERTAKER

Riley Thomas, Wood Street

UPHOLSTERERS

Cremonini James, Oxford Street
Riley David, Oxford Street

VARNISH MANUFACTURER

Waldron Samuel, Cambridge Street

VETERINARY SURGEON

Kent Charles, Union Street

WHEELWRIGHTS

Bennett Thomas, Hallfields
Bradley John, Hall Street, Hallfields
Elliott John, Hartshorn Street
Nash William, Oxford Street

WINE & SPIRIT MERCHANTS

Peck William, Oxford Street
Taylor Elizabeth (Mrs.), Church Street

WINE & SPIRIT VAULTS

Bache David Jones, High Street
Crooke Charles, Church Street
Holton Benjamin George, High Street
Hyde George, Church Street
Plant Henry, Oxford Street
Plant Walter & Co. Church Street
Tomkys John Law, Lichfield Street

WIRE MANUFACTURER

Rollason D. & B., Bradley works

The People Who Lived in Staffordshire Series

1. **HANLEY**

This book is intended for the genealogist researching family history in the Potteries town of Hanley in the English county of Staffordshire. Geoffrey Hugh Lindop has compiled this book by extracting information from the Staffordshire Post Office Directory of 1864 and presenting it in a modern font. In doing so the genealogist or local historian will find this booklet easier to read than the original. An alphabetical listing by surname of the influential inhabitants may assist in family history research but in 1864 they had to pay to be included in the directory so poor families are not listed. A classified section (not in the original) has been added so the amount and type of commerce in 1864 can be judged. The book is completed by a description of Hanley and since it was written in 1864 provides an eye-witness account of the town.

The Peopole Who Lived in Hanley in 1864
by Geoffrey Hugh Lindop
ISBN: 978-1501043222 . This is a 'Print-on-Demand' book published by Mercianotes and printed by CreateSpace available from all good bookshops or in case of difficulty from the printer's website:
https://www.createspace.com/4789045 where a full description can be found.

2. **BURTON -ON-TRENT**

A similar treatment is given for Burton-on-Trent in 1864, which includes an 'eye-witness' account of the town written in 1863.

The People Who Lived in Burton-on-Trent
by Geoffrey Hugh Lindop
ISBN: 978-1511616805. This is a 'Print-on-Demand' book published by Mercianotes and printed by CreateSpace available from all good bookshops or in case of difficulty from the printer's website:
https://www.createspace.com/5419510 where a full description can be found.

For details of all Mercianotes titles visit

www.mercianotes.com

Nancy Lindop's Genealogies Series

Nancy Lindop who died in 2005 aged 96, spent about 50 years as a genealogist tracing not only hers, but other people's family trees. A founder member of the South Cheshire Family History Society, which met in her house in the Shropshire village of Woore. Nancy delighted in sharing her research and helping others in their quest to find their ancestors. As well as collecting information from local libraries and record offices she also had an extensive library where books were catalogued into the English counties of Shropshire, Staffordshire and Cheshire and it is mainly from these three counties that the subjects of her research lived. Her son, Geoffrey, has converted her hand-written notes into book form and analysed her original research with his personal computer - a technology unavailable to Nancy.

1. LINDOP

This book is intended for the genealogist researching family history in the Family tree Charts of the Lindop Family from the 13th to 20th centuries. The family is traced from its origins at Lindop in Derbyshire to locations across England and Wales up to the beginning of the 20th century.

2. HAMPTON AND GRINDLEY

Hampton lists details of the eighty-six members of the Hampton family that are recorded in the Mucklestone Parish Register between 1555 and 1649. Mucklestone (or Mucclestone as it is sometimes spelt) is situated in north Staffordshire about 4 miles north-east of Market Drayton. Details of the Hampton family that lived in the Shropshire parishes of Adderley, Berrington, Claverley, Condover and Whittington are also included.

Grindley features the 66 members of the family who lived in north Shropshire and the research has covered 45 parishes in that area. Also included are surnames with the variant spelling: Grimley, Grindall, Grindley, Grindle, and Grinlye.

3. BAKER, FURNIVAL, JONES AND SHUKER.

IFifty-five members of the Baker family who lived in North Shropshire, South Cheshire and North Staffordshire are described

In the same area, but more localised around Mucklestone, can be found the Furnival Family 105 members of which are described together with 31 in-laws.

The Jones Family of Woore only extends to only 19 members.

Nancy has researched the Shuker family of North Shropshire in 45 parishes and found 128 records of the family.